Photosynthesis

Blooming in the Dark

Ana Castillo Jiménez

PHOTOSYNTHESIS

Blooming in the Dark

Photosynthesis: Blooming in the Dark

Copyright © 2025 Ana Castillo Jiménez

All rights reserved.

ISBN-13: 979-8-9888048-3-3

Cover design and illustrations by: Ana Castillo Jiménez

Ana
Castillo
Jimenez

To those who have placed a pebble on the path

that has led me to where I am today—

Your kindness, patience, and encouragement

have shaped my journey in ways words can scarcely express.

I am eternally grateful.

Prologue

What if I were to tell you a story or two?

Are they false or true?

I'll give you a clue:

In this universe,

every creature, every plant,

and every element plays a part.

In this intricate game of nature,

there is a hidden truth

within every heart.

Each being holds a light deep inside

capable of shining blindingly bright,

though many are unaware of its presence.

Often, we wander through life's maze

seeking a light, seeking a reason to exist,

not realizing that the shadows we face

hold the answers to all our questions.

Life is a journey of endless possibilities

where everyone solves their own mysteries.

Every road traveled is unique,

and every road taken is correct.

They all lead to the present moment.

Keep your eyes open and you might see

that everything is as it should be,

this is all part of your story.

Chapter I: Disorientation

Nestled next to countless siblings,

I sway in the midnight breeze,

my pappus brushing theirs.

Together, we form a white crown

for the dandelion we call Mother.

Her stem, strong and steady beneath us,

is an anchor to this meadow.

I've watched her bend and sway

under countless currents,

only to straighten again,

determined and unbroken.

"Move over,"

mutters a sister,

her feathery strands

tickling my edges.

"You're blocking my view,"

another protests.

Being one seed out of many
means I always have company—
hundreds of puffballs pressed closely.

Each one part
of something greater.

I shift closer to Mother,
who sighs contentedly,
flowing with the night.

A pulse, gentle and steady,
moves through her stem—
a reminder that life hums
even in seeming stillness.

The night winds are getting warmer
and I can't help but wonder
what's around the corner.

I stretch my pappus,

straining to see,

but the wind interrupts—

a gust makes me retreat.

Shadows come out to play

while the day is away.

Questions swirl like storm clouds:

What if the winds bring a tornado?

What if the sun forgets to return?

The scent of grass and soil sours

as my body tenses with distress

and I get lost in what ifs.

What if I get hurt or lost?

What if everything goes wrong?

Thoughts spin in circles

until Mother leans in,

rocking me gently.

6

"Take a deep breath with me,

darling,"

she whispers.

"You are where you are meant to be,

my brave, beautiful seed.

You are safe here with me.

Nothing here is scary,

there is no need to worry.

There are only new ways to see.

Slow down for a minute,

and shift your perspective."

Her voice, warm as sunshine
disperses the storm in my mind.

Tucked within this blanket of pappi,
I know all will be alright.

I focus on Mother's presence,

on the warmth that lingers

from my siblings' touches.

Their soft brushes against my surface

tickle me as darkness presses closer.

Breath by breath,

my body calms

slowing the swirling chaos,

grounding me in the moment.

I shift my perspective,

and the meadow awakens anew.

The what ifs dissolve into thin air,

like mist evaporating under the sun.

The world sharpens around me

as my senses focus.

Owls hoot to one another
from the cloaked embrace of trees,

crickets buzz their tireless tunes
from beneath a flower's bloom,

fireflies flicker and flash
sharing secret signals,

worms slither and slide by
digging their way through the grime,

and nearby, a stream conducts
the crashing of multiple waves,

each one flowing in an effortless way
that I long to experience someday.

There is beauty in the darkness

when I pause and listen.

Ancient trees speak of change,

their voices riding the midnight wind.

                                        "Seeds like you,"

they murmur,

                                        "are meant to fly."

Their words hold stories

about the journeys of heroes,

about a whole new world.

Their call to adventure

is as strong as the flutter

of a butterfly's wings,

capable of setting in motion

a storm that will change

my life's trajectory.

I absorb their tales,

each more vivid than the last,

speaking of lands beyond imagination

where so much can happen

once I dare to leap into the unknown.

Hours pass as I drift on their words,

picturing lands out of this world.

They send messages through the breeze.

                                        "Dare to explore,"

they whisper through rustling leaves.

                                        "Journey beyond."

They speak of golden lands

beneath ruby red skies.

Like sirens, they lull me in,

their stories impossible to resist.

I let their voices hypnotize me

as their words dig into my memory.

11

They speak of freedom,

of flight,

of transformation.

Though I do not sleep,

dreams come easily.

Despite lurking storms,

I envision lands

made of sunshine,

where stars glow day and night,

where the air shimmers with light,

where grass glitters like gold,

where there is much to behold.

Each word they offer is a seed

taking root inside of me,

growing into a longing

for something

that is meant to be.

They say there's magic and mystery,
that there is much I have yet to see.

They say life has more for me
beyond my current reality.

"Freedom awaits,"

the wise ones reassure me,
their ancient boughs speaking of centuries
spent watching seeds like me take flight.

"Trust your path,"

they encourage,
urging me to let go and surrender,
to let myself be swept away.

"Become,"

they conclude, a single word
that echoes through my being like thunder.

To become— not just to exist,
but to transform, to grow
into something greater.

I want to be more than just
one seed among many,

I want to go somewhere
where I never worry.

Life here is good, undoubtedly so,
but my heart wants to go

beyond this meadow,
beyond all I know.

I wish to go somewhere new
where life will have a different hue.

I don't know if wishes come true,
but I don't know what else to do.

Birds sing soulfully

as they celebrate dawn's return.

The sun approaches from the horizon,

as it always does.

Its warmth touches me,

and with it comes doubt.

The what ifs return:

What if the stories aren't for me?

What if I'm not meant for journeys?

The trees fall silent,

their whispers fading,

but their stories linger,

rooted in my brain.

I find myself swaying

between what is

and what could be,

between past,

present

and future.

I feel the pull of their messages,

soft echoes playing in my head:

Become.

The word repeats in my mind,

over and over again.

Become,

become—

I can't help but think

that perhaps…

there is something wrong with me.

Should I not be content
with the fragrance of flowers,

with the lullaby of leaves,
and with the buzzing of bees?

Should I listen to the trees?
Should I leave?

Am I going crazy?

This is the only home I have known,
this is the place where I was sown and grown.

This must be where I belong,
I just need to keep playing along.

Daylight spreads across my surface,
a gentle warmth that is inviting.

My pappus unfurls slowly,
reaching instinctively upward.

I anchor myself in the allure
of this brand new day.

I focus on breathing,
taking in my surroundings.

Surely, this is where
I am meant to be,
in this meadow
with my family.

But the stories have taken root,
and they refuse to be forgotten.

"Watch carefully, little ones,"

Mother's voice interrupts my thinking

as clouds begin to pass overhead.

"Smell as the air grows thick.

Listen for the soft rumbles

moving through the earth.

Nature speaks

to those who are willing

to pause and listen."

The meadow is alive

with the distant growl of thunder.

A warning from the horizon.

Hours pass, as does the storm.

My siblings and I are tucked in,

trusting that Mother

will take care of everything.

This life is paradise,

what could be better than this?

What more could I possibly want?

Why would I want to leave?

As the sun dips lower,

shadows creep closer,

and the whispers return.

Trees begin to speak,

their words a steady rhythm.

'Fly.

Trust.

Become."

Once again, I find myself

balanced between longing and fear.

The sun slips away,

and the voices get louder,

filling the air with wonder.

The trees speak of destiny,

of all that I could be

once I set myself free.

They share stories of whom and what

I am meant to find and become:

                                                            "Radiant."

They describe

a beautiful blossom,

a vessel of light,

laden with pollen,

brimming with life,

pulsing with power.

Their words dig deeper into my soul,

as if they've always belonged.

They plant seeds and visions

of what my life could be,

of a new perspective

beyond what I see.

The trees whisper of the gale,

the current that will carry me

to something greater.

For this journey there are

no belongings to gather,

no farewells to utter—

for a seed like me

it is as simple

as letting go.

As night starts to fade,

a new voice rises—

not from the trees,

but from my head.

Many of the stories

seem too adventurous for a seed.

One sailed across oceans,

another rode on a wild beast,

one discovered untouched territory,

another gave rise to a new species...

The stories blur into impossibility,

the tales suddenly seem silly,

too mythical to believe.

Their magic dims

as uncertainty gets a grip.

The storm I've felt looming

continues to speak,

its voice like my own,

but distorted.

Are you sure?

she whispers.

Do you truly believe

you can become

something extraordinary?

The tales I once found enchanting

now seem like childish dreams.

What if the trees lied?

"Mother?

How do you stand so strong?"

My voice shakes,

seeking steady answers

amidst the storm that is growing.

Her response ripples through us all:

"Strength isn't about standing rigid,

but in knowing when to bend.

You don't need to fight the winds,

feel your way through them.

Whenever storms arise,

trust they will pass.

Everything will change,

it's just a matter of time.

Remember, my precious seeds,

you carry all answers within."

Her words settle over me,

and I let out a breath

I didn't know I was holding.

I am unsure of what to do,

and that is okay.

It is okay to pause,

to rest as I wait

for the light

of a different day.

For now,

I choose to stay

with Mother,

with my siblings.

Maybe someday,

when the winds are right,

I will let go.

But for today,

this is where I will grow,

this is where I will remain.

But nature has plans of her own.

The wind speaks in her own language,

with her wild and ancient tongue,

and this dawn, she roars.

Morning arrives not with the soft breath

of a gentle zephyr,

but with the fierce command

of a gale wind.

It begins as a whisper,

threading through the grasses,

gathering strength as it rises

up Mother's steady stem.

Soon, it becomes a howl,

a chorus of chaos.

The trees say nothing

as Mother Nature bellows,

every strand of my pappus

humming with her force.

The air is thick
with the scent of spring,
sharp with hints of rain.

Around me, my siblings quiver,
their tiny forms trembling
against my own.

Then, all at once,
they are gone.

I am torn from Mother's embrace,
the warmth of her touch vanishes,
replaced by the cold hands of destiny.

I am taken from my cradle,
from the only home I have known,
without any warning.

This is not a tranquil departure—
it is a violent awakening,
a sudden plunge into havoc.

One by one, my siblings and I

are plucked from the crown

and into the sky.

We leave our home behind

as we learn how to fly.

Our parachutes deploy

as we are flung

without so much as a goodbye.

We scatter like white stars

against the soft blush

of the morning horizon.

The meadow shrinks beneath me,

becoming just another memory,

a collage of greens and golds

blurring before my eyes.

Twirling around the meadow

I dance with the wind,

the time spent with my family

has come to an end.

My siblings are nowhere to be seen.

I cling to the memories we shared

as distance pulls us apart.

Spinning into the endless blue,

I wonder if they, too,

heard the trees' lullabies.

I wonder if they, too,

want to scream and cry.

Suspended between earth and sky,

I am caught in a liminal space

where dreams and nightmares merge.

The wind shows no mercy,

tossing me higher, faster,

into a future I cannot predict.

Life has left me perplexed,

tumbling through the unknown

with no clue of what is coming next.

My thoughts tumble as wildly
as my trapped body,
questions swirling in the wind:

Did anyone see us leave?
Will anyone search for us?

We're being taken away
and no one is stepping in.

Are we too small to be helped?
Too insignificant to be noticed?

Besides Mother,
we likely won't be missed.

What is going to happen?
Where am I going?

My world dissolves into a puddle
as I enter a landscape I barely recognize.

Branches lash at me
as I hurl onward,
each near miss
making my heart race.

Gone is the world I once knew,
with its sweet perfume of flowers,
and the comforting crashing of waves.

In their place are acrid fumes—
a metallic stench that stings my senses.

Below, monstrous machines roar,
their shining bodies hurtling
across endless gray rivers.

Their glowing eyes pierce the morning mist,
watching me with mechanical indifference.

This place is mayhem incarnate.

Life moves at a pace
that makes my head spin.

Everyone and everything
rushing, running, racing
against time itself.

The meadow never knew
such urgency.

Each bee took its time
buzzing from bloom to bloom.

The trees took their time
growing each limb.

The birds took their time
singing and humming.

The waves took their time
forming and flowing.

Here, everyone is running
out of time, always in a hurry.

Everything is too fast,
I am lost in the frenzy.

Time seems to be
everyone's enemy.

Suspended in the currents,
I soar for what seems like ages,
like an albatross adrift in a storm.

I am caught between two worlds—
between the one that I left behind
and the one that I am meant to find.

The sky is vast and unpredictable,
the ground below an alien world.

All my senses strain past their limits,
overwhelmed by the constant input.

It is so hard to think or breathe

with so much happening.

My body is no longer my own.

The sun traces an arc across the sky,
following an unseen rainbow.

I follow its rays across its route,
riding a current that won't let me go.

The reality of my situation
becomes clear all at once:

my siblings are gone,
and I am completely alone.

This is all wrong,

this is not where I am meant to be.

I am a seed—

I am not meant to fly.

I do not have wings,

I am not destined for the sky.

Mother's words echo in my mind,

rising above the noise:

> *Nothing here is scary,*
>
> *there is no need to worry.*

> *There are only new ways to see.*

I close my eyes,

take a trembling breath,

and calm the storm within.

> *You don't need to fight the winds,*
>
> *feel your way through them.*

The frenzy begins to blur,

the rushing world slows.

The sprawling landscape below

becomes something new—

every patch of grass,

every sliver of earth,

turns into a possible place

for my becoming.

Somewhere down there
awaits a new beginning,
a place where I will take root.

The wind, as if hearing my thoughts,
begins to ease her grip.

Her screams quiet
as I am guided downward
with surprising gentleness.

I drift toward the ground,
toward the world I understand,
toward solid, steady land,
toward where I am meant to be,
toward a familiar reality.

Chapter II: Propagation

I settle onto a small mound of dirt,

a haven of green tucked amidst the gray.

The cool touch of the earth

is a welcoming hug,

greeting me as I return

from my long journey.

I breathe deeply,

inhaling the musty perfume

of soil and damp roots,

the comforting scent of growth

coming from the ground itself.

My body softens,

what remains of my silken pappus

rests against my side

as the hum of motion

is replaced by stillness.

This place—this park—
is unlike the meadow.

A city surrounds me,
buildings stand to my left,
fences stretch to my right.

There are no fireflies in sight,
but the city lights flicker
with their own signals.

As I rest in this new foundation,
my gaze lifts, drawn upward,
to the endless sky from which I fell.

The sun begins her slow descent
into the horizon's waiting arms.

That's one constant that remains,
night still follows day.

For the first time,

there are no pappi

to block my view—

no siblings close by

to obscure the evening sky.

It stretches endlessly,

bigger and more boundless

than I ever imagined.

The lights seem to dim,

setting the mood in this park.

My sight is locked upon

the sparks from the sun's arc.

Twilight begins its show,

bathed in a golden glow.

Light spills out from the heavens,

decorating the sky with ribbons

of oranges and reds

that pulse and spread.

Clouds become glowing embers,

their edges kissed by fire,

each hosting unique hues.

They ripple with colors

that shift and bend

with every passing second.

The horizon is a cauldron of flames,

overflowing with life

that refuses to be contained.

The fire spreads upward, outward,

each tendril of color

reaching toward me,

as if daring me to ignite.

The fire finds my heart.

A spark catches.

Small and hesitant at first,

but growing with every beat.

I let it spread,

welcoming its warmth

as it races through me,

illuminating every corner

of my being.

The sky shines ruby red,

it is as if I am floating

in a river of embers.

I inhale deeply,

letting the waves wash over me

as the flames keep me warm.

I want to let myself burn,

burn,

burn.

The sky, adorned in her evening attire,

is a masterpiece crafted

by Mother Nature's hands—

the same hands

that brought me here,

the same hands

that shaped the universe.

As the spectacle unfolds,

a thought begins to grow,

tentative yet determined,

like a leaf reaching for light.

What if the ancient trees were right?

Even though I am grateful

for this delightful display,

some small part of me

remains unconvinced.

Is this where I will grow?

Or is this just a stop along the way?

The sunset offers no answers,

but my gut does—

a quiet murmur that tells me

there is more coming.

Before I can fully embrace this new place,

the ground beneath me begins to quake.

It starts softly, with a faint vibration,

but quickly grows into a rhythm,

an approaching force that dispels

the enchantment of the evening.

Paws pound against the ground,

each impact sending tremors

through the soil and into me.

The thumps echo louder and louder,

a beat of unpredictability

that shakes me to my core.

I brace myself,

my tiny form tightening

against whatever is coming.

thump,

Thump,

THUMP,

THU—

In one violent,

inevitable instant,

the thump is upon me.

Weight crashes down.

I am forced deep into the soil,

swallowed by darkness.

In the space of a heartbeat,

my world collapses.

Earth pushes in from all sides,

slowly suffocating me,

grains scrape every surface.

Each layer of dirt

is a fragment

of what came before.

Decomposed leaves,

broken roots,

ancient stories

containing history.

I am buried alive,

left to wonder

what has happened to me?

I am lost in a tomb

with no sense of who I am.

The soil refuses to yield,

the way out is concealed.

From the heights of the sky
to the depths below,
I have fallen through the world
and down the rabbit hole.

From the freedom of flight
to this crushing cage—
how quickly life can change.

I try to extend what remains
of my bruised and battered pappus,
to reach, to stretch,
but it only meets resistance.

My chest grows tighter
with every breath,
stones scrape my surface—
some sharp as tiny blades,
others smooth and worn.

The pressure builds,
each passing moment
becoming heavier than the last.

53

Broken root fragments

brush against me—

ghosts of lives

that no longer exist.

Dread seeps

into my being,

slowly at first,

then all at once.

A full-on storm

forms in my mind.

I burst into panic.

There's no oxygen left
to fuel my inner flame.

The ember that once burned brightly
is reduced to ashes, snuffed out
by my impending doom.

The darkness is absolute,
thick and smothering.

It fills my mind
as my thoughts
twist and tangle,
spiraling downward.

I am lost,

I am nothing.

I am too small,

too fragile,

too powerless.

This is it,

this is the end.

It is hard to see,

hard to think,

hard to breathe.

I am just a seed—.

why is this happening to me?

Thoughts spiral like leaves

caught in a tornado,

whirling faster and faster

until individual worries

blur into one.

This is all wrong,

this can't be happening.

My mind bends and twists

like the branches of a willow.

I can't do this,

I don't want this.

Vines of dread

tighten around my heart,

squeezing until there's nothing

but a hollow, aching void.

"Somebody, anybody,"

I cry into the silence,

"please help me."

But there is no answer.

I close my eyes and retreat

into the depth of my being,

but it makes no difference.

The darkness has found

its way inside.

I let the soil press in,

let it fill the spaces

where light once lived.

There is no trace

left of my family.

Where their pappi once brushed mine,

there is only cold, lifeless earth.

I am alone.

Truly, utterly alone.

The shadows seem solid here,

thick enough to hold,

empty enough to devour me whole.

In this silence,

I am left

with only my thoughts—

spiraling darker, heavier,

pulling me into an abyss

I cannot escape.

I don't like this new place,

it is nothing like the meadow.

I miss the sun's warmth,

my family's love.

Here, life is only an echo

of what once was.

59

Clouds pour into my mind,

casting images of failure,

each imagined scenario

more terrifying than the last.

My shell feels too tight,

my body all wrong,

as if the very essence of me

is coming undone.

The silence pulses—

a presence of absence,

an entity so tangible

it seems to throb

with a phantom heartbeat.

I am barren, like a flower

after its last petal has fallen,

stripped of everything

that made me *me*.

From the shadows in my mind,

a voice torments me,

quiet but insistent:

Perhaps this was all

you were ever meant to be—

a single seed, tiny,

without purpose,

without destiny.

Perhaps you were never

meant to be anything.

Fear creep further into my soul,

swallowing every spark of hope.

Why me?

Why am I here?

Why even bother?

The soil meant to nurture me

snuffs out my spirit.

I teeter on the brink of oblivion.

I want to believe

I can reach and grow tall,

but I am so small,

so inconsequential.

The voice inside

pulls me closer to the edge.

Why not let go?

Why not give up?

I stare into the abyss,

its emptiness tempting,

and wonder if this

is my true end.

The ancient trees' promises—

of becoming, of trusting, of growing—

wither within me.

The seeds they planted

shrivel and collapse

under the weight of my despair.

How can Mother Nature have plans

for something as fragile as me?

I get lost in my head,

in my forests of habits,

in the storm that rages.

The world above

is a distant memory,

its colors and sounds

no longer part of my story.

Life is like a cruel trick

played by the hands of fate.

Here, in the underbelly of the world,

time seems to pause.

Somewhere in the darkness.

shadows stir.

There is a sound—

so faint,

I almost miss it.

The gentle scratch of movement.

I strain to hear it.

In the absence of sight,

my other senses come alive.

The silence I thought absolute

begins to transform.

A critter digging—

the legs of an insect scratching softly

as they carve a path around me.

Tiny vibrations pause to inspect,

antennae brush against my shell.

Curious, they linger for a moment,

before continuing their journey.

A fellow traveler

through this subterranean world.

Other sounds join in:

the soft buzzing of a beetle,

the vibrations from burrowing animals.

65

The dark isn't empty—

it was just waiting

for me to listen.

Life surrounds me,

invisible but persistent,

teeming with motion.

Worms leave nutrients

where they tread.

Roots sing out,

as if trying to lure me in.

Insects go on about their day,

as if everything is okay.

An entire universe exists

just beneath the surface.

Here, in the embrace of shadows,

life unfolds in intricate patterns,

connected in ways unseen.

Each creature around me

has mastered the gloom,

not by fighting it,

but by feeling their way through.

They don't resist the dimness—

an inner light guides them.

Far beneath the surface,

I hear the call of fungal threads,

each carrying messages

to and from places.

They speak of nearby worlds,

of nutrients exchanged,

of needs fulfilled,

of symbiotic success.

With a deep inhale,

the fear that bound me

begins to loosen.

Something within me shifts—

like the first rays of sunlight

breaking through storm clouds.

The darkness that trapped me

now reveals its secrets:

a universe of beings

thriving without light,

finding their way

by other means.

With an exhale,

I relax.

The tension I carried

melts away like snow in the spring.

I let the rhythm of this world

teach me how to move.

Each layer of soil
has a story to share.

Fragments of fallen leaves
speak of seasons passed.

Crumbled bark and roots
share tales from decades ago.

Each grain of dirt
is full of microscopic life,
carrying traces
of growth and decay.

I listen to the world,

until I hear a new vibration—

subtle at first,

a faint tremor,

a rhythm,

a pulse.

Thump,

thump,

thump,

thump-

Chapter III: Germination

The thumps grow stronger,

a rhythm that fills the earth.

It is a familiar beat

that I welcome with a smile.

My heart,

once restless,

now calms,

falling in sync

with the tempo.

Each raindrop plays

a note, a letter, a sign,

crafting a message,

a call to awaken.

I remain still,

my senses alive

as I listen.

The raindrops continue their beat,

sending ripples through the soil.

Each droplet carries purpose,

seeping through layers of dirt,

creating unique vibrations

that establish a new foundation.

Between the soil particles,

tiny pockets form,

miniature puddles.

The earth no longer scrapes;

it soothes, its cool touch

damp against my shell.

Water reaches me,

not just a substance,

but a force—

life in liquid form.

Like messengers on a mission,

the molecules whisper:

"You are not buried,

you are planted."

The rain's cool kiss is a revelation,

as if each drop holds

a piece of the sky

from which they fell,

a fragment of the universe.

The ground swells,

softening and shifting,

as energy floods my cells.

Water coats my surface

patient and persistent,

seeking out the tiny pores

hidden within my shell.

Moisture finds its way

through invisible gates

that have waited lifetimes

for this exact moment.

The refreshing touch of water

unlocks memories planted within—

of who I am,

of what I carry,

of where I come from:

I am a seed, a vessel of energy,

holding the blueprint

to create life

and shape my destiny.

This is my invitation from the universe,

my token to participate

in the grand game of life.

And I choose to play.

Something stirs within—

a strength long dormant,

waiting for this awakening.

My cells stretch

as ancient instincts

begin to unfold.

Each drop of water

is filled with a promise,

with a message from the universe:

"Keep going."

Yet, doubt lingers like fog.

It seeps into the edges of my mind

through the distorted voice:

What if you can't become

what nature intends?

What if you can't

trust your instincts?

The desire to break free

from the darkness is potent,

yet the direction is elusive,

the way forward unclear.

I long to rise,

to find my place beneath the sky,

yet I am lost in a catacomb,

uncertain if I can breakthrough.

From the depths of memory,

Mother's voice emerges.

Her words ripple through me:

"You are where you are meant to be,

my brave, beautiful seed."

Her voice settles over me

like a weighted blanket.

I take a deep breath,

letting the memory sink in,

letting it ground me.

I breathe in the scent of rain,

inviting calmness into my body.

My outer coating begins to soften,

its rigid protection yielding

to the flow of life.

Pressure builds within,

as energy radiates

across my entire surface.

Beneath, ancient machinery whirs—

molecules dance and break apart,

enzymes activate,

proteins unfurl

like leaves reaching toward sunlight.

Mitochondria power on,

ready to create,

to grow,

to evolve.

Nutrients stored deep within

begin to flow freely,

streams of potential coursing

through my small form,

guiding the intricate transformation

with molecular precision.

Something deep inside expands,

an instinctual force emerging

from an age-long slumber.

Water reshapes me,

reminding me that I am

capable of flowing

into new ways of being.

Though the darkness still holds me,

I no longer resist;

I simply listen.

Life flows around me,

within me.

My mind replays the trees' words,

"Dare to explore."

Life is a game I get to play
until my very last day.

Dead ends are inevitable,

but so is the chance to redirect,

to regroup, to try again.

This is not chaos;

it is a chance for growth.

Each effort is guided

by an inner knowing—

a pull toward the light.

My cells are at work

each one dividing,

carefully playing a role

within my body.

My shell gives way.

Not in defeat,

but in a deliberate act

of metamorphosis,

splitting along invisible seams

made for this.

The first root cell awakens.

It presses against my softened walls,
searching for its emergence point—
where shell meets soil,
where potential becomes reality.

The crack begins small,
a hairline fracture
slowly spreading outward.

The urge to move
overwhelms me.

I feel the pull,
the need to reach, to push,
to break free
of what once contained me.

It is blind faith—

trust in life's game—

that compels me forward.

As minerals from the soil

flow into me,

their ancient strength

infuses my being.

A silent, wordless knowing

spreads through my skin:

The time is now.

Slowly, deliberately,

I shed the limits

of my former body.

I stretch beyond my boundaries.

With a lunge,

a reach into the unknown,

I trust the pull of life.

My root emerges,

white as moonlight,

delicate as silk,

yet strong enough

to pierce the void

between what was

and what will be.

Tentative at first,

then bolder,

it seeks an anchor

in this new world.

A shoot follows,

slender and green,

filled tenacity.

It seeks the surface,

it yearns for light.

Root hairs sprout like curious fingers,

testing, tasting, seeking

paths of least resistance.

Each one stretches outward,

drinking microscopic films of water

that cling to the soil particles,

absorbing them through osmosis.

First one root, then another,

driven by the unshakeable belief

that there is more waiting.

Life is a game,

and though I may not

know the rules,

I know I must play.

My roots push deeper,

building me up.

Each tendril an anchor

to a new possibility,

drawing strength

from Earth's elements.

Memories flicker like fireflies.

I remember the meadow,

the beauty waiting up above.

I recall the closeness of my siblings,

and whispers carried in the breeze:

"Freedom awaits."

These recollections are vivid,

saturated with color and light.

They rekindle my desire for daylight,

reigniting old embers in my heart.

The flames of memory grow,

small sparks transforming into wildfires,

an unstoppable force urging me upward.

With newfound willpower,

I focus my energy on the sun.

Hour by hour,

day by day,

my shoot presses onward,

and my roots dig deeper.

This is not a reaction;

this is a response—

a deliberate act of growth.

To emerge is to believe,

to believe is to know

that I am part

of something larger,

a game programmed

by the cosmos.

Shadows may loom,

hiding challenges,

but they also hold

great treasures.

To grow is to rise

through the unknown,

to stretch beyond

pain and doubt.

In this hidden land,

untouched by sunlight

yet filled with life,

I feel a tug from a place

I cannot see,

but know exists.

My soul holds a burning desire,

a longing for dreams that have yet to be,

for the destiny taking shape

right now within my body.

The fire within glows brighter

illuminating the path ahead.

I explore the soil, learning to read

the map of history all around me,

remnants of what used to be.

Traces of life long ago

continue to withstand time,

watching new forms

come and go.

Above me, faint murmurs

filter their way through the soil—

the muffled sounds

of the world above.

Raindrops patter against leaves,

and somewhere, a bird calls,

its melody faint and distant.

Each sound, each sensation,

reaffirms my resolve:

It does not matter what lies ahead,

or what challenges I may face.

What matters is that I keep going,

that I keep trying.

I am writing the narrative of my story

as I craft a journey of ascent.

I press forward.

The rocks beneath my roots
are solid and steady.

They are not obstacles,
but steppingstones.

I pass through chambers within the soil,

tunnels of air and movement.

Earthworms twist and curl,

their bodies gliding through the dirt.

Their movements aerate the earth,

softening the path I am on.

Life continues to hum

quietly beneath the surface,

a steady rhythm of renewal.

The fire within me burns,

its light unwavering.

With each push forward,

I grow closer to my destination.

Above, the rain still pounds,

its beat echoing through the soil,

signaling the way out.

The ground drinks

with an endless thirst.

Each layer of dirt

fills and swells,

as if the earth itself

is ready to sprout.

I stretch a new root,

searching for stability,

reaching for the next steppingstone,

but I find no purchase.

The soil beneath me is no longer firm,

no longer a trusted foundation.

It is too wet,

too saturated.

Each raindrop hammers the earth,

softening what once felt solid,

until the world

begins to shift.

A slow slip at first,

barely perceptible—

then a deep groan

rumbles through the soil.

Then—

everything gives way.

The dirt loosens all at once,

liquefying into thick mud.

My roots, once anchored,

are wrenched free,

ripped from the earth.

They stretch, strain, and fight

to hold on to what they can.

One by one, they snap—

each one a broken promise.

I

s

l

i

d

e

a

w

a

y

.

The world glides

into a churning tide.

Mud rushes around me,

dragging me along

its torrential trail.

I am caught

in its wrath,

tumbling,

twisting,

tripping

through the darkness.

I reach out

for something to steady myself,

fighting against the current—

but there's nothing to hold on to.

The mud engulfs me,

pressing, pulling,

spinning me deeper

into the void.

I have no sense of direction.

No way forward,

no way back.

Just an endless descent

to the bottom of nowhere.

100

Chapter IV: Natural Selection

There is no up, no down—

only the endless pull

further underground.

I am weightless,

suspended in a slurry

of dirt and debris.

Cold seeps into my body

as my dreams dissolve

right before me.

The world is swirling in a storm

both within and without.

Each twist and turn

batters my body,

bruising, pressing, grinding

me down.

I am caught in a new game,

one I never wanted to play.

The rules are unknown,

and the only certainty

is that I'm losing.

The fire within me flickers,

dampened by the flood.

I am lost.

Adrift in the shadows.

Drowning in the unknown.

Wild thoughts prowl my mind,

their edges sharp as thorns,

their whispers full of venom.

They tear into me,

each one jagged

with doubt.

Was it all a lie—

the promises of growth,

the dreams of radiance?

Did the ancient trees deceive me

with tales of transformation

for a seed that was never

meant to flourish?

Or

am I too weak

to claim the destiny

they swore was for me?

104

Questions wrap me into a knot,

like ivy choking a sapling,

each tendril squeezing tighter,

and tighter,

and tighter—

until even hope

feels like a betrayal,

like a joke

played by the universe.

I am tired.

So tired of fighting,

of believing in fairy tales

spun from the breath of old trees.

Their whispered promises

now mock me through the waves.

105

Why me?

My mind rages silently,

boiling over with frustration

as the darkness closes in.

Why was I chosen for this journey

only to be abandoned here?

Why gift me dreams of flight

if I was meant to suffocate

in this lightless night?

My fury burns hot,

but hollow.

There is no fuel left

to stoke the embers.

I am exhausted.

What's the point of fighting

when every struggle

only sinks me deeper?

I resign to the darkness,

ready to let go,

to let the silence

take me whole.

The storm in me quiets

in resignation.

With an exhale,

I surrender.

Like evening frost,

a numbness

spreads through me,

quenching my will

to keep going.

Perhaps this is my true destiny—

not a glorious transformation,

but a quiet fading

into nothing.

The current carries me,

the tide swallows my form.

I resist nothing.

I give into the darkness

that is now inside of me,

letting the void win.

I leap into it,

into oblivion.

There is nothing but shadows

filling the darkness,

brimming to the edge with it.

It is all I can see,

all I can hear,

all I can feel.

I dissolve,

falling into the black hole

within my soul.

A descent into vast,

empty nothingness,

a pit in the middle of space

where time does not follow.

The silence stretches wide,

endless.

I become the void.

For a moment,

it feels like the world

has stopped—

but I know it hasn't.

I am still here.

I am still breathing.

Time passes,

the mudslide slows.

The world stops spinning.

The rush, the terror, the fight—

all of it is replaced

by stillness.

I am too tired to analyze,

to question, to push.

For the first time since my burial,

I do not try to grow.

I do not try to escape.

I simply exist.

I no longer know

what I should feel,

what I should do,

what I should think.

I only know

that I am still here.

My thoughts rise and fall,

like a stream losing momentum,

slowing to a trickle.

Sounds come to me.

The hum of the world beyond,

never resting,

a machine that never ceases.

Yet here, in the void,

I remain.

I focus on my breath—

on the only thing

I can still control.

In...

Out...

In...

Out...

I wait for the storm to pass,

for my mind to clear

until it is empty,

like a fertile field

waiting to be sowed.

This is who I am

beneath the stormy skies—

emptiness,

a blank observer

in this universe.

Within the void, I cultivate

a garden of my own design,

sowing seeds of my destiny.

I feel the sun within me rise,

illuminating this space

where shadows linger.

Within my heart,

I construct a refuge

untouched by doubt—

a place to take shelter

when storms come out.

In this inner paradise,

the air is rich with the scent

of possibility.

My roots deepen,

and my spirit flows.

My mind is free

to imagine all

that could be.

Distant waves mirror

my breath's steady rhythm.

Soft grasses caress my skin

as the wind sings lullabies.

Sunlight filters through

unseen branches,

casting warmth upon me.

I let apricity embrace me,

trusting that everything

unfolds as it should.

I rest.

In this space,

I am neither lost nor found;

I simply am.

I picture the blossoms yet to bloom,

the vibrant colors that will one day emerge.

Life unfurls within me,

telling me that I am growing

where I am meant to be,

doing what I am meant to do.

I do not need to force

the seasons to change,

I do not need to chase

the light meant for me.

I tend to my inner home,

one built not on certainties

but on curiosity and trust.

I wait patiently,

knowing the universe moves in cycles,

and that even the longest night

yields to sunrise.

My heart's garden blooms

with flowers of acceptance,

their petal soft as surrender,

their fragrance sweet as peace.

Here, I am rooted

in the quiet joy of being.

This moment,

this breath,

is enough.

I plant seeds of sunlight, wind, stars,

and of the sky's touch.

I recall the owls, crickets, and creatures

waiting just above the surface.

This shelter within

is a secret garden

where I wholly belong,

now and always.

In this place,

the sun always shines,

and storms of worry

cannot reach me.

My mind is tranquil,

like a still pond

reflecting endless blue.

Thoughts ripple across the surface

before returning to eternal calmness.

In this space, waves flow effortlessly

through me, teaching me to bend.

Birds sing for the sun,

and the trees' whispers

bring ease to my soul.

The air is rich

with the faint fragrance

of wildflowers,

soothing all my worries.

Time stretches

into something limitless.

In my inner vastness,

stillness, silence, emptiness,

something awaits birth.

A spark.

Small at first,

barely more than a flicker

from deep within my core,

yet it holds everything

I hope to be,

all I long to become—

radiance.

Its light does not struggle in the darkness,

but rather exists within it.

It flashes with belief,

with the knowing

that possibilities still exist,

even when I cannot see them.

I choose this light.

Not the storm of thoughts

that once raged uncontrolled,

not the darkness

that once consumed me whole.

I focus my energy on this spark,

growing it into an ember.

Its unwavering glow leads me—

not with words, not with signs,

but with something deeper,

something truer.

Intuition.

As the light within me blooms,

something else does, too—

something that seems

too good to be true.

A new voice speaks

from within me,

from within my heart.

A new perspective.

She whispers:

just keep going,

keep moving forward.

This is not my end.

Even when everything crumbles,

even when I get swept downward,

even when loss feels inevitable—

this spark remains.

I can keep going.

There will be an after.

> "Whenever storms arise,
>
> trust they will pass.
>
> Everything will change,
>
> it's just a matter of time."

I just need to hold on.

To breathe.

To take one step,

then another.

Darkness stretches before me,

full of questions

I cannot yet answer,

paths I cannot yet see.

It holds unpredictable obstacles,

more challenges and tests.

My body tightens,

every instinct screams

stay where you are,

stay where it is safe.

But is staying safe?

Here, where I have curled in on myself,

where the air has grown stale,

where my roots, once strong,

have begun to dry and whither?

No.

This is not safety.

This is slow decay.

This is the quiet erosion

of everything I could be.

And so,

I reach.

Not because I am fearless,

but because staying where I am

is the only thing more frightening

than the unknown ahead.

I may stumble,

I may slip and slide,

but I will not wither.

I will not stay buried

beneath my own fear.

I move,

because to grow,

I must.

I don't need to see the whole path,

only the next step,

illuminated by my radiant spark.

With each step forward,

its light grows—

brighter,

steadier,

stronger.

Within this void,

I am never lost.

I am becoming.

Even if my whole world

turns inside out,

if everything I know

dissolves before me,

if tides rise

and foundations crumble,

I will still have me.

Still have this body,

this vessel, this home,

crafted by the hands

of the universe herself.

Generations of knowledge

coded into my being

through the patience of time.

Every cell, every breath

that sustains my life,

is a miracle of existence.

Trusting my potential,

I extend my roots,

thanking each one

for the support they provide.

Even if they break,

even if they fray,

I know they will mend

with a bit of patience.

My stem pushes through soil,

through rocks and debris,

carving the path

that will set me free.

Stepping out of my mind,

I am absorbed by my surroundings.

There's the distant murmur

of water threading its way

between grains of dirt,

pooling, shifting,

feeding the unseen.

The earth pulses with life,

there are mysteries waiting for me.

The rich scent of earth is all around,

deep and full of memory.

There is subtle heat

from decomposing leaves

breaking down into the soil,

heat that is now entering my body.

I absorb its energy,

a force, a truth,

that nothing can shake:

there is still beauty in the darkness.

A beetle taps against a pebble,

a morse-code message

for the universe.

A cricket hums a tentative note,

practicing scales for a song

not yet ready to be sung.

A colony of bacteria,

glowing with bioluminescence

like an underground constellation,

seems to wink at me,

pointing me onward.

131

Earthworms continue digging tunnels,

their bodies press gently

against one of my battered roots,

soft, deliberate, reminding me—

I still have company.

Beyond all this life,

I sense something deeper,

something more than ancient.

I listen.

It is as though everything has aligned

for the universe to say:

"Everything is going to be okay.

You are not done yet."

Two ants pause their work nearby,

their antennae brushing together in greeting.

A millipede stops near my stem,

sending out tiny vibrations to my core.

All around me,

conversations seem to carry

from all sorts of creatures

going on about their lives.

                        "There is a way out,"

they seem to say.

                 "There is always a way forward."

Each handful of soil

holds its own universe

teeming with life.

Roots stretch and sigh as trees grow,

conversing in frequencies

I begin to perceive.

They come together in harmony,

an intricate lattice

of subterranean support.

Everyone has a role,

everyone has a purpose.

I am not alone,

I never have been.

I am part of a community

that has thrived for centuries.

A young root from a nearby tree glows,

its tip phosphorescent with fungi.

"We are all connected through invisible lines,"

she explains, stretching slowly toward me.

"Every root eventually intertwines.

In the absence of sight, we find our way

through the code written in our DNA.

Your body knows the way to go,

you are led by an inner flow."

In this hidden world,

I learn to see a new light—

not the piercing brilliance of the sun,

but a softer, quieter glow,

the light of shared existence,

of lives interplaying

in an endless cycle

of giving and receiving.

Each being has a spark

waiting for its time to shine.

In this collection of soil,

death and life mix so closely

they are no longer separate,

but one continuous motion,

one infinite rhythm.

Mother's voice plays in my head,

"Nature speaks

to those who are willing

to pause and listen."

Every overheard conversation,

each brush with underground life,

is a new seed planted within me.

I water them with wonder.

I warm them with acceptance.

With every new discovery,

my inner garden is fertilized.

Instead of fighting the darkness,

I let it teach me its secrets.

I begin to understand:

my thoughts are like the weather—

they come and go

through rain and shine,

but beneath them,

I remain,

grounded.

I learn to navigate by touch,

to trust in what I cannot see,

to grow in directions

I never expected.

The mud that once felt empty

now brims with potential,

with endless possibilities

waiting to unfold radiantly.

Earth settles around me,

my roots stretch and reach,

trusting I will find what I need.

The wisdom of the trees

takes on a new meaning.

They never promised an easy journey—

only that it would be worth it.

I sense the sun pulsing far above,

reaching through layers of earth.

My shoot stretches upward,

blind but certain,

drawn by something deeper

than sight.

The sun's pull reminds me

that light and shadow

are partners in growth,

each shaping the other

through nature's game.

The voices in my head—

the whispers of doubt,

the echoes of fear—

fade into the background

like ripples settling on a still pond.

I focus my attention

upon the voice within my heart.

Keep going.

You have made it this far.

One more push, one more stretch.

Just keep growing.

You can do this.

You are doing this.

The doubt loses its edge.

Not an enemy, but an old habit—

one I no longer water.

I'm done feeding the fear

that has kept me rooted in place.

Instead of tensing and retreating

when faced with the unknown,

I feel a surge of energy,

a readiness to explore.

Perhaps I am lost,

I think,

but being lost has led me

to more adventures

than I imagined.

I listen to my surroundings

and feel into my body.

The soft rustle of life

fills the silence.

I dig deeper,

finding purchase

in understanding

that even here

—*especially here*—

I am growing.

The stories I once thought

were about escaping

were never about running away.

They were maps—

guides to transformation.

I am held by the earth,

not as a prisoner,

but as something cherished,

something supported,

as I shape myself

into my unique form.

I am getting stronger,

getting closer.

I am further along today

than I was yesterday.

With every root grown,

I defy the pull of gravity,

reaching for warmth.

Days pass like water

filtering through the soil,

each one whispering lessons

of patience and perseverance.

I grow slowly but surely,

gathering strength in my stem,

wisdom in my roots,

and light in my being.

There are still days

when the darkness feels heavy,

when every movement

feels like carving through solid stone.

But even then, I know—

this resistance is reshaping me,

teaching me to be more resourceful.

I don't need to know the way,

I remind myself.

I just need to stay curious
about what's possible in this game.

Each obstacle becomes a question:

How else might I grow?
Which way shall I go?

What else might I become?
What will this all be for?

Bacteria shimmers nearby,

their glow a soft reminder

that light can exist anywhere,

even here, even now.

As I reach,

I sense a difference in the soil—

a slight coolness,

a hint of openness

I have never felt before.

I stretch upward.

My tender stem,

used to the give of the soil,

meets something new.

Something unnatural.

Something that does not yield.

Not soft earth.

Not shifting grains of sand.

Not ancient, sharp rocks.

This is something else.

Cold.

Hard.

Artificial.

A surface that does not

soften under rain,

that does not invite life.

Impenetrable.

The skin of a world I had forgotten,

one with towering structures

and restless motion.

Chapter V: Adaptation

I cannot pass.

There is no way to proceed.

For a moment, I falter.

All my growth, all my striving—
could it have been for nothing?

The voices in my mind rise,
shouting over one another,
each one echoing a fear I've faced before.

It's over.

You have reached your limit.

You will never break through.

They rattle in my brain
like seeds in the wind,
a storm of doubt
clouding my skies
with flurries of worries.

Fear bubbles up,

welling from unseen springs,

rushing through me

like a dam breaking.

I let the voices vent their fear,

releasing the pressure

of every what if and every worry.

And when they are done,

I breathe.

In...

Out...

And retreat

to my garden.

When challenges arise,

my mind reacts

before my body remembers.

Old ways try to reclaim me,

voices from a past

I've left behind.

They claw at my core,

trail up my stem,

grip me in place,

root me in distress.

Then—

another breath.

In…

Out…

I become a river,

letting my emotions

flow through me,

not against me,

not around me,

not bottled within.

I feel their weight,

their heat,

their jagged edges—

but I also feel them leave,

becoming lighter with each release.

Stillness follows.

This darkness isn't a void;

it's a sanctuary.

where everything begins again.

No matter what is lost,

no matter what changes,

I still have me.

And that is enough.

That is everything.

My body knows.

She grows, she evolves,

she listens to the rhythm

of the universe.

She speaks the language of life itself.

Every breath,

a conversation with the wind.

Every heartbeat,

an echo of the earth's vibration.

My only job is to listen.

I am whole.

Not because of what I have,

but because of who I am.

And I love that about me.

The words rise unbidden, simple and true.

I love that I am sustained—

by my body, by the earth,

by the abundance that surrounds me.

I am supported by the energy

flowing through me,

ancient and new all at once.

I feel it then—

this endless energy,

something untamed and electric,

pulsing with the power of life itself.

It reminds me that I can keep going.

I will keep going.

Because I am all that I need.

I am part of all that is.

The light I once sought from above

now emanates from within.

I no longer chase it;

I carry it.

Resting within this sanctuary of self,

I witness darkness and light intertwine,

transforming fear into flowering,

turning dead-ends into rebirth.

Seeing the beauty within my soul,

I see beauty in everything.

Even here,

where there is nothing to see.

The world hums around me,

a song I haven't always heard

but that always plays.

I reach out a root,

tracing the cool surface

of the concrete above me,

feeling its story.

The weight of time

that crafted its existence.

Each piece of this world

is molded through intention,

each holds something

for me to witness,

to appreciate,

to love.

The universe has never been careless.

Every crack, every grain,

every unseen detail—

is perfect in its own way.

And I—

I will never be alone.

The earth holds me.

The stars, though hidden,

still shine above me.

Creatures move in the shadows,

living, breathing, reminding me

that life carries on,

that I am part of something vast,

something connected.

My heart swells with gratitude

for every stone on my path,

for every whisper of life around me,

for every moment that reminds me

that even as I navigate this darkness,

I am never lost.

I am here,

where I am meant to be.

"Journey beyond."

I hear the trees whisper.

Their stories were never

just about reaching skyward.

They were about embracing

every layer of life,

about understanding

that true strength

is not found above ground,

but in the balance of darkness and light,

of solitude and connection,

of stillness and growth.

I am learning

to embrace all of it,

to trust the unknown,

to reach when I cannot see,

to grow when I do not yet understand.

I rest

in the glow

of my love.

I do nothing.

I do not move,

I do not reach,

I do not push.

I simply exist.

The world outside carries on—

temperatures drop and rise,

the earth turns,

life stirs.

But I remain still.

I listen.

To my breath,
to the earth,
to the soft hum of my body
as she tells me what she needs.

No urgency.

No expectations.

Just presence.

In this eternal now.

Time ebbs and flows,

carrying moisture through the soil,

allowing life to shift

and settle in its own rhythm.

The world continues its game,

and I remain rooted within it.

I rest until the ache in my soul softens,

until the weariness in my spirit lifts.

I reset until my energy is full,

no longer driven by desperation,

but by the gentle nudge of readiness.

Somewhere deep within me,

my small, steady spark speaks.

The voice within my heart murmurs,

it's time.

I stretch,

I breathe,

I trust.

I am ready to try again.

The first steps into the unknown
are always the hardest.

Reaching out blindly,
unsure of what my roots will find.

Will they grasp something solid,
or slip through a crack?

Will the ground beneath me hold,
or crumble in the blink of an eye?

I do not know.

And that terrifies me.

But even so, I keep going.

I remind myself—

everything will change.

Time is a quiet revolution,
a shifting tide that rolls dice
and scatters obstacles
like leaves along my path.

And though I stumble,
though I may fall,
I also rise.

This situation is not bad;
it is simply different.

Another page in a story
still being written,
a path that curves,
revealing new landscapes
at every turn.

I continue,

following the light I cannot see,

but know is waiting.

My small spark continues to grow,

illuminating the sky within me.

I crawl along the edge of the stone sky,

knowing this barrier, too, shall pass.

The strength I've found in every challenge

when I wanted to quit but didn't

has carried me here.

This is just another threshold,

another chance to choose

who I am becoming.

The current of life moves around me,

and for the first time,

I do not fight against it.

I bend,

I sway,

I adjust.

I do not break.

A voice seems to rise from the earth itself,

soft as soil after rain.

Mother Nature speaks,

a whisper woven

from stones and roots,

from water and sky:

> "You are home,
>
> you never left it.
>
>
> Home is not a place to be seen,
>
> but an experience to be felt.
>
>
> It is not a location to be found,
>
> but a feeling to be created.
>
>
> You are safe,
>
> held within my embrace.
>
>
> You are loved,
>
> a precious life in the universe."

Her words cradle me.

In this embrace,

my body softens,

relaxing into the knowing

that I am supported.

Even here,

pressed between

earth and concrete,

I am exactly where

I am meant to be.

Above me,

minerals seep through the concrete,

tiny gifts from the world beyond.

I absorb them gratefully,

drawing strength from their essence,

fueling my transformation.

No matter what happens,

I am supported by Mother Nature.

She provides,

she nourishes,

she guides me through this journey.

I am safe.

I am loved.

There is no need to worry.

I am meant to grow,

to reach,

to evolve.

And I am doing so—

at my own pace,

in my own way.

It is only a matter of time.

As I navigate this unyielding ceiling,

something blooms within me—

an awakening,

a remembering,

coded in my cells.

A shift,

imperceptible yet profound—

a release of control.

I move with ease and clarity,

my body fluent in the language

of Mother Nature.

There is no fear here,

only the freedom

of being my own destination.

I belong in this soil,

I am part of this world.

My roots grow stronger

with each breath,

seeking sustenance

in the smallest of spaces.

Where others see barriers,

I find openings,

transforming limitations

into possibilities.

My body becomes my guide,

each cell a repository of wisdom

passed down through the ages.

I learn to trust the subtle pull of intuition,

in the quiet voice that says—

Grow here.

Rest there.

Reach this way now.

My gut knows the path

better than my thoughts ever could.

And so, I listen.

I listen to my roots tingling

as they find water and nutrients.

I listen to the stillness

as I continue to grow.

Above me, my stalk stretches,

pressing against the foreign surface,

searching for any weakness,

any crack or crevice.

Even though this concrete sky

is a manufactured horizon,

I do not despair.

Here, in this liminal space—

between earth and artifice—

I face my greatest test.

Not of strength.

Not of endurance.

But of faith.

The questions rise:

Do I surrender to this barrier?

Does my story end here?

Or do I trust in the force

that drives seeds into trees?

The same force that taught

stars to burn,

planets to spin,

flowers to track the sun.

I close my eyes.

I return to the meadow
I have built inside
with patience and love.

Here, my small light continues to bloom,

drawing energy from my roots,

glowing like a sunrise,

bathing my garden in light.

Each petal is a memory,

each leaf a lesson,

each stem a testament

to how far I will go.

I have already arrived

at my true destination.

I have become

all that I was meant to.

Led by inner radiance,

I etch along the perimeter.

I do not force the path,

I let it reveal itself.

I move as life moves—

slow, steady,

aligned with the unseen.

Though my reserves dwindle,

my resolve grows stronger.

I am no longer the seed

that trembled in the dark.

I have bloomed internally

through the spark in my heart.

The earth hums to me,

a gentle song of existence

echoing through every particle of soil,

through every thread of root:

"Trust your path,

trust your growth."

My cells remember this call—

it is an inner compass

that needs no sight to guide,

wisdom far older

than thought or memory.

This compass, steady and true,

guides me through the darkness

better than eyes ever could.

This knowing lives in my roots,

speaking through my forming shoot,

coming from the branching trees—

ancient as starlight,

certain as gravity,

clear as water.

181

I navigate by instinct,

letting my body guide me

in ways my mind cannot comprehend.

Each day, I learn

to trust my instincts a little more,

reading the soil,

sensing the unseen.

Sometimes, I surge forward,

pushing upward with all my strength,

reaching toward the warmth I sense above.

Other times, I rest,

my roots drinking deeply

from the wisdom of the earth,

listening, learning, allowing the stillness

to shape me as much as movement.

The trees above have grown

in this way for centuries,

trusting the seasons,

letting the wind teach them

when to bend

and when to stand tall.

Every twist in the path,

every unexpected turn

is part of the pattern,

part of the perfection

of becoming.

Every root that reaches out,

every leaf that forms,

every cell that divides

is guided by light.

Growth is a steady rhythm

between effort and ease,

between reaching and resting.

What once seemed like limitation

becomes an invitation

to grow in unique ways.

Light can flourish anywhere—

it is not something to chase

but something to become.

My first true leaves begin to form,

tiny but determined,

already knowing how to catch light

that doesn't yet exist.

My roots stretch further,

threading through pathways

until they connect to a network,

the hidden web of intertwined roots.

As I deepen my connection

with the world beneath me,

the mycelium networks carry messages

of the earth's endless patience,

of persistence beyond all obstacles.

"There is a way,"

they whisper.

"Always."

This knowing lives in my roots,

speaks through my forming leaves.

In this space between worlds,

my cells divide and multiply

with intention,

each new growth

appearing exactly where it is needed.

I am both confined and free—

held and supported

by the very barriers

that once seemed to trap me.

I understand now—

strength is found in surrender,

growth in acceptance,

and life in the stillness

between seconds.

Time moves differently here,

not in days or seasons,

but in the deepening of roots

preparing for what is to come.

Moment by moment, I make my way

tending the landscape of my body.

Every choice,

every pause,

every movement

is part of my becoming.

Through the steady strengthening

of my expanding form,

my inner garden flourishes.

The light within me grows stronger,

feeding on the peace I have cultivated within.

When rain seeps through from above,

I welcome its cool blessing,

carrying whispers of the world

I am destined for.

Far above,

the sun's presence comes and goes

with each passing day,

a distant warmth that calls to me

through layers of soil.

It speaks of possibilities,

of light waiting to be discovered.

I listen—

not just with my mind,

but with my entire being.

What I once mistook

for anxiety,

for hesitation,

for uncertainty,

I now recognize as energy

waiting to be channeled.

Through trial and error,
I learn the rhythms of being—
when to push and stretch,
when to rest and absorb.

I test my limits mindfully,
amazed by my capabilities.

I learn from the quiet efficiency
of the earthworms,
from the patience of pebbles
as they remain silent and still.

I stretch my roots deeper,
unfurl a little further,
and remember the sun's embrace
as I build strength in the unseen.

Channeling my energy with care,

I direct growth with intention.

Here, a new root.

There, a stronger shoot.

Always growing, never forcing.

An elder root creaks along the cement:

"Young one, do you know why

some of us grow so deep?

It is not despite the obstacles,

but because of them.

Each stone we meet,

each patch of soil,

tests our creativity.

Let your imagination

show you the way.

Anything is possible

given enough time of day."

I listen as the earth speaks to me—

through the life around me,

through the rhythm of water,

the shifting temperature of soil,

the pull of something greater than I can name.

Then—

a change.

A different texture.

A slight shift in the surface.

I pause—

sensing it with every fiber of my being.

My leaves press forward,

tasting the difference,

following the instinct

I now trust without question.

A crack.

Thin—

barely there,

but unmistakable.

A passage.

A way through.

A gate to another world.

Chapter VI: Photosynthesis

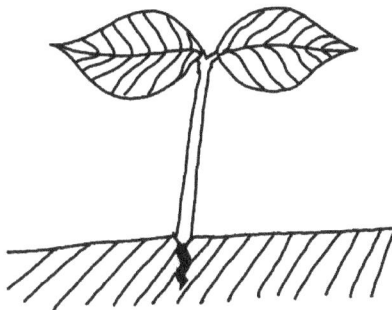

With deliberate care,

I direct my growth upward,

pushing through the narrow passage,

reaching toward the world

where my journey started.

Gravel scrapes my sides,

but I barely notice.

Every fiber in my being knows—

this is the moment I have been reaching for,

the moment that has been waiting for me.

The earth gives way,

the last layer of stone

loosens its stubborn grip,

and I emerge.

For a single,

breathless moment,

I expect to be blinded by the sun,

drenched in golden warmth,

welcomed by the light

that helped me make it

through the darkest night.

But the world is not bathed in daylight.

It is night.

I release my breath.

I blink,

startled by the openness.

No ceilings of soil,

just space—

infinite and endless.

The sky above is vast and deep,

spilling like obsidian ink.

As I gaze, a star blinks into view—

then another, and another,

until the atmosphere ignites

with shimmering constellations,

distant fires burning ages ago,

turning the sky into a luminescent ocean.

Each flickers like a firefly,

glimmering softly

against the night's velvet embrace.

So many more than I remember,

so much brighter.

Their light pierces the darkness,

each one a tiny sun,

a distant echo of something eternal.

I have made it.

For so long,

my world has been dim,

my existence wrapped in shadows.

But now I see—

darkness was never an enemy.

It is the reason stars shine so radiantly.

And oh—

the cool night breeze.

It brushes against my leaves,

a caress both familiar and new,

carrying fragrances I had forgotten.

The air is alive with the scent of spring,

whispers of blossoms I have yet to meet,

electric hints of life thriving unseen.

My leaves tremble,

not with fear,

but with the sheer joy of feeling.

I stretch them up and out,

reaching for the perfect spheres

sparkling right above me.

I want to catch their light,

to hold their glow in my cells,

to let the stars know

that I have made it,

that I am here.

And though they remain

forever out of reach,

their radiance fills me

with a warmth that rivals the sun.

Their light is not something I must touch to feel.

The Milky Way stretches wide,

a river of starlight,

a path through the cosmos,

whispering there's always a way.

I drink in the beauty of it all—

this sky, this moment,

this universe that has always been here,

waiting to be seen.

Each star feels like a heartbeat,

a cell within the cosmic body,

each constellation a story

etched in lumens across the heavens.

Galaxies spiral overhead,

infinite and unknowable,

yet somehow familiar,

as if I have always been a part

of their celestial game.

The moon rises.

She is half-full tonight,

but her glow is complete,

soft and silver,

a beacon of reflection.

Even partially shadowed,

she radiates a presence

that seeps into my being,

calming and energizing all at once.

The weight I have carried,

the doubts that lingered,

lift with the tide of her glow.

The night air caresses me gently,

and though the sun has yet to rise,

I no longer fear its absence.

Here, in this moonlit patch of pavement,

beneath this canopy of stars,

I do not feel small.

I feel vast, endless,

like I belong here as much as the stars.

Time slips away as I gaze skyward,

my leaves turning upward,

drinking in the light that has traveled

unimaginable distances to reach me.

The stars mirror the light

I have found within.

Their glow reminds me:

light persists.

We are all connected—

stars and seeds,

darkness and dreams—

each playing our role

in this grand cosmic narrative.

Through the depths of the earth,

through silence and stillness,

through storms and shadows,

I have learned—

light never truly fades.

It only waits to be remembered.

Darkness, too, has its gifts,

teaching me to find light

where none could be seen.

And now, beneath this endless sky,

under the watchful glow of the universe,

I add my own small brightness to the world,

the only way I know how—

I grow.

I have found my way,

not by conquering the shadows,

but by learning to shine within them.

Night yields to sunrise.

With gentle grace,

a slow unveiling of color,

soft and gradual.

The first hint of light

kisses the horizon,

a barely-there glow,

a sigh before the world wakes.

The sky shifts from obsidian to deep violet,

to the softest shades of indigo and blue,

painting itself in one-of-a-kind hues.

Birds break the silence,

a single note at first,

then another, and another,

until the air is alive

with a greeting for the light.

Each note vibrates through me,

a song of life carried by the wind,

one I now sing along to.

I feel it in my stem,

in my roots, in my breath—

a signal passed from the trees,

through the roots beneath me,

carrying the quiet understanding

that all things move in harmony.

Dewdrops capture light,

each one a prism of possibility.

Shadows stretch and yawn,

softening from black to gray..

Then—

there it is.

The first true sunbeam

finds its way to me,

and my entire world ignites.

It is like being born again,

like taking my first real breath,

like waking from a haze

into something more vivid and real.

Warmth spills over me,

soaking into every surface,

stitching together the scars

left over from my journey,

binding them with energy.

My chloroplasts awaken,

hungry for light,

aching for this golden fuel.

Photon by photon,

energy floods my veins,

a silent alchemy within.

Sunlight becomes sugar,
sustenance absorbed from the sky.

Breath by breath,
I transform—
turning light into life,
creating air for others to breathe.

This is what I was made for.

This cosmic exchange,
this invisible miracle
that has been happening
since the dawn of existence.

I drink deeply from the sun,
stretching wider,
reaching higher,
craving more warmth, more sky.

Life is solar-powered,
life is light transformed,
life is energy exchanged.

I breathe,

and the trees breathe with me.

I give,

and the world gives back.

The air around me

hums with motion,

invisible currents of oxygen

flowing between leaves and lungs,

between plant and animal,

a silent exchange of breath and being.

My cells vibrate,

each one a tiny powerhouse,

each one playing life's game.

Breath by breath,

I weave deeper

into the network of life.

I am not just part of this world—

I am shaping it.

The sun feels like Mother's love,

like the universe's embrace,

like coming home to myself

after a long time away.

Each ray is a soft whisper of welcome,

a reminder that I have always been

a beloved piece of existence.

Stars continue to shine day and night,

even when no one is looking.

So do I.

I sway with the breeze,

finding grace in every movement.

Some days bring golden warmth
that wraps around me like a shell.

Others, thick blankets of clouds
that dim the world to muted grays.

Some nights are calm and moonlit,
their silver glow a soothing balm.

Others roar with thunder,
wild, electric, and unpredictable.

I no longer fear the shifting weather.

The wind sings to me,
its voice woven with tales of distant places,
of resilience and change.

The rain does not weep;
it nourishes, washing over me,
quenching my thirst
and feeding my roots.

The storms do not threaten;

they play, their wild energy

a reminder that life

is not meant to be lived in stillness.

Energy builds within me,

expanding and contracting

like the breath of the universe,

guiding me forward.

My roots,

deepened by the darkness of my past,

anchor me firmly between earth and sky.

No matter how the winds howl

or the rain pours,

I remain steady,

held by the strength I have cultivated.

On cloudy days,

when the sun plays hide and seek,

or on stormy nights

when the air shivers with cold,

I turn to my inner garden—

the sanctuary I carry within myself.

Here, light always shines.

Here, warmth is endless.

Here, I am home.

No storm,

no creeping shadow,

can take the glow I carry.

Every challenge

has only made my light brighter.

I tend to my inner world often,

watering the thriving roots of joy,

planting new seeds of potential.

In this tranquil space,

waves still crash upon golden shores,

the wind carries the scent of wildflowers,

and the sun always sets

in colors without names.

This place is me,

the part of myself that blooms

regardless of the world's whims.

My perspective shifts one more,

like leaves turning toward the light.

Where once I asked,

What if?

I now wonder,

Why not?

Curiosity blooms in me,
a second set of leaves,
fresh pages in my story.

Each question leads
to a new possibility.

Rain becomes a celebration,
clouds become a spectacle,
the wind a playful partner,
the sun a welcoming spirit.

I play with shadows,
flirt with sunbeams,
let my leaves ripple
with every passing breeze.

I continue to grow,

not just from survival,

but from the pure joy

of being alive beneath the sun.

With each passing day,

I stretch taller,

grow stronger,

dig deeper into the earth

that has always held me.

Leaf by leaf,

I reach for the sky,

stem strong and steady,

my spirit light.

I don't chase the future,

nor do I cling to the past.

I exist fully in this moment,

trusting in the flow of life.

My taproots grow more muscular
with each passing day.

My leaves develop deep lobes,
jagged with strength
drawn from deep underground.

Their edges are as sharp
as a lion's teeth.

The rich soil feeds my growth,
its earthy scent rising
with each gentle rain
that glows on the pavement.

I feel buds forming,
ready to emerge.

Everything is changing—
my mind, my body,
my surroundings.

Knowing my heart's intentions,
I set forth on a new direction,
gently guiding my actions
with my careful attention.

I focus on connections
while not seeking perfection.

Life is full of inflections
called natural selection,
a series of reactions,
a chance for redirection.

The universe is a kind teacher,

providing me with chances

to learn more about myself

and the world I inhabit.

The wind carries the sweet perfume

of nearby grasses

along with the warmth of spring.

It whispers through my leaves,

bringing messages about pollination

and weather changes.

I listen with my whole being.

Three buds emerge from my stem

and reach for the sun,

yearning to touch the light.

They open slowly, deliberately,

their petals unfurling to reveal

a brilliant yellow

that mirrors the sun's radiance.

Each flower is a gathering of florets,

thousands of potential futures

blooming as one.

They open at dawn.

The air shimmers with light

as pollen drifts,

carried by the gentle wind.

The world around me

thrums with life.

Rabbits thump nearby,

their burrows nestled in the tall grass.

Ants march in orderly lines at my base,

their tiny feet leaving microscopic trails in the soil.

The air itself feels alive,

saturated with the scent of growth,

with the subtle fragrance

of leaves, petals, and earth

mingling beneath the sun's glow.

Everything I need

is flowing toward me.

Butterflies and bees
visit throughout the day,
their wings stirring small breezes
that make my petals sway.

The air hums with their gentle music
as they gather my golden gifts.

An orange-winged friend
flutters around my flowers,
her delicate feet
touching down like soft kisses.

My pollen feeds countless creatures;
I am a vital part of the ecosystem.

My flowers continue the cycle of life,
contributing to the world in ways
I once only dreamed of.

I have done well.

I have made new friends,

and I have seen so much.

But I'll keep my eyes open.

There is always more to discover.

Our corner of the world

fills with unique perfumes—

grass, soil, and dozens of different flowers

creating a collage of scent and color.

Everything comes together

in perfect harmony:

the way light plays on dewdrops,

the dance of butterflies,

the gentle swaying of grass stems.

Even here, surrounded by concrete and steel,

nature finds a way to create beauty.

Looking at the leaves on a nearby tree,
I know they've been here
much longer than me.

They teach by example,
swaying in the breeze,
rooted in patience,
thriving with ease.

Though each leaf is different—
one chewed by a caterpillar,
another still growing,
one turning yellow at the edges—
they all work together
supporting the same living being.

The tree doesn't depend on any single leaf,
yet needs them all to thrive.

Even once fallen, trees continue to give,
their trunks creating homes,
returning nutrients to the soil,
feeding life's endless cycle.

Branches reach for the sky,

whispering warnings of falling forests,

and approaching droughts.

Seasons aren't as they used to be,

and the changes will only grow more extreme.

Yet they tell me not to worry.

What will happen next

is not up to me.

It never has been.

Control was always an illusion.

Mother Nature—

she's been building something bigger,

something we can't fully see

from where we stand.

And maybe that's the point.

I've spent so long trying to map the constellations,

chasing echoes vibrating between stars,

digging through layers of soil

in search of something greater.

I believed clarity would bloom

if I just dug deep enough,

if I peeled back every layer

of silence and shadow.

I have stood at the edge of knowing,

trembling with the need to pull back the veil,

to see the mechanism behind every sunrise,

to name the force that pushes me upward,

to pin down my place in this universe.

226

But what if some things
are meant to remain hidden?

Maybe magic rests in not knowing,
in the quiet thrill of possibility,
in the gentle ache of curiosity unfulfilled.

Every moment feels like a discovery,
each day a chapter written in ink
that dries before my eyes.

What if the unanswered questions
are the universe's way of saying,

"Trust me,
I've got this."

There is beauty in the way

life insists on being a surprise,

how it shifts and swirls,

refusing to be anything but itself.

Maybe the unknown is a gift,

a place where anything can happen,

where possibilities stretch beyond

what we think we need.

Tomorrow awaits with its secrets,

a story I have yet to read,

and I've come to love

the steady unfolding—

the chaos and the calm,

the way wonder finds me

even when I have stopped looking.

Maybe my purpose is not to decode

the mysteries of the universe,

but to flow with them,

to follow their rhythm,

to hold my heart open wide

and trust in the unseen

as I find joy in the story

told one breath at a time.

What is life if not a marvel of mystery?

My purpose isn't to reach the stars,

but to bask in their glow

as they rise and fall.

And is it not enough

simply to feel their light?

To let the magic remain,

untouched by reason,

to let wonder linger

where it wishes to be?

I release my need

to resolve the riddle,

to tear apart the cosmos

into digestible pieces.

I find peace

in the not knowing,

in the bliss of simply being

a traveler savoring the journey,

trusting the path to lead where it will,

learning at last to enjoy the story

as I rest in Mother Nature's hands

that have been holding me all along.

Days pass in a rhythm of sensations:

the warm caress of sunlight,

the cool touch of evening,

the gentle brush of passing creatures.

My flowers close at dusk,

their golden treasures folded safely

against the cool night air,

resting until morning's call.

No two days are the same—

no two skies alike.

Even though I am in the same place,

watching the same horizon,

the world is always different.

Each day, brand new things

happen for the first time.

Clouds bloom and dissolve,

the sun spills gold in ways

it never has before,

and never will again.

It is a game that never stops updating.

I could spend a lifetime watching

and still never see it all.

And isn't that beautiful?

Isn't that exhilarating?

Yes, it could be scary,

even overwhelming,

but it is also thrilling—

a gift wrapped in infinite possibility.

Because it could be anything.

Truly anything.

Just when I think I know,

just when I start to understand,

everything shifts—

and that's amazing.

This is the universe at work,

the quiet hum of her algorithms,

the sacred rhythm of her expansion.

Unpredictability and change,

coded together with infinite care,

designed so that nothing,

not a single thing,

ever remains the same.

And yet—

it all comes together just so.

All the pieces align,

falling into place

within the puzzle,

crafted by hands

that have shaped stars and seas,

mountains and time itself.

How breathtaking,

the way everything changes.

How incredible,

the way I don't need to hold onto it,

don't need to control it.

I can just trust.

I can place my worries in Her hands,

let her do what she has always done.

I get to witness her artistry.

I get to enjoy it.

What a gift.

What an incredible opportunity.

Thank you.

My petals begin their graceful retreat,

signaling the close of one chapter

and the impending rise of another.

The day exhales its last breath

as the sun meets the horizon.

The air grows heavier,

quieter,

as the world waits

for the unveiling.

Chapter VII: Blooming

Then—

she rises.

The moon returns,

like I knew she would.

She doesn't always visit,

but tonight,

she graces the world in full.

She lifts herself above the earth,

ascending with effortless grace.

She bares everything,

peeling back the darkness

with her gentle glow.

Her light spills over the cement,

a cool silver sheen

that clings to every blade, every leaf,

painting the world in a serene glow.

I cannot look away.

Her presence stirs something within me.

I see myself in her—
a mirror hung in the sky,
a quiet companion
through the endless cycles of life.

Even when she offers
only a sliver of herself,
she gives all she can.

Even when hidden from sight,
she remains faithful
to her rhythm of retreating and returning.

Her light is not hers alone;
it is borrowed, reflected, shared—
just as mine is.

Her glow feels familiar,

a resonance deep in my being—

it's the same light

that pulses through my stem.

This light is the signature of the universe,

a subtle spark that threads through all things.

It shows the way through life's game,

holding the answer for every question.

I bask in her glow,

not to take, but to remember:

I, too, am a spark,

capable of illuminating the dark.

The moon and I—

we are reflections, reminders

that even in the deepest night,

there is always light waiting to shine.

242

My sense of self expands
as I begin to form seeds,
new roots grow
in the garden of my being.

From one to many,
each one a dream
creating a unique narrative
never to be repeated.

Potential exists within me,
unspoken stories waiting to be born.

I am surrounded by lives
I will never experience,
stories I'll never read.

And yet, they are all here,
sharing this moment,
adding to my narrative.

The blades of grass,

the leaves, the seeds, even the clouds—

each one holds a piece of me,

and I of them.

Part of me remains the same,

part of me is always becoming.

I am both rooted and scattered,

both whole and growing.

In this perfect contradiction,

I find my truth.

I am here only to be.

Not to conquer obstacles

or carve meaning through stone,

but simply to breathe in

the gift of this moment,

to rest in existence.

My purpose isn't sculpted by achievements,

not forged from striving or ascending,

but found in the unfolding of life,

in the soft rhythm of simply being alive.

And that is plenty.

What grander purpose could there be

than to witness the world

through the lens of my being?

To feel the sun melt across my skin,

to marvel at the shimmer of stars,

to gaze upon a sky painted in twilight,

to listen to the wind's songs.

What if I am here not to understand,

but simply to admire

the beauty stretched before me?

What eons of evolution

have shaped into this very moment,

this perfect now that will never again repeat.

Mother Nature holds me in her hands,

guiding my breath

to match the swaying of her seasons,

teaching me to soften,

to simply exist.

Maybe growth and learning

are simply byproducts of living,

not the purpose of life itself.

Maybe I am not meant

to pull myself apart

in search of greater meaning.

It is enough to simply exist.

The point of the game

is simply to play.

To feel the earth beneath,

to breathe the air held by leaves,

to swim in the golden light of morning,

to rest with the stars with eyes full of wonder.

I am a creature born

from stardust, soil, and sunlight,

a witness to the world sculpted by centuries

into a planet that cradles life in all its forms.

Each moment,

each challenge,

each joy—

they are all invitations.

Opportunities to grow,

to learn,

to feel,

to experience life in all its depth.

And isn't that incredible?

That I get to be here,

that I get to play this game,

to move through this world

filled with mystery and meaning.

The trees whisper stories of roots

entangled deep in the earth,

mountains hold secrets of fire and ice,

rivers flow with memories

of rainstorms and stillness,

the ocean roars of creation and calmness.

This planet,

this reality,

this universe—

what a gift it is to exist within it.

To wake up and to stand beneath a sky

that is never the same twice,

to feel, to wonder, to become.

Even the hard moments—

even the ones that feel unbearable—

they too are part of the design.

They shape me, refine me,

remind me of my strength,

of my resilience,

of my infinite capacity to transform.

This is the universe's beautiful pattern—

not just change, but growth.

Not just movement, but evolution.

I am constantly shifting,

learning, adapting, expanding,

just as the stars,

just as the tides,

just as all things do.

And I love that.

I love that I get to witness it,

to be part of it.

I love that I am here,

living this story,

playing within this vast,

ever-unfolding masterpiece.

So I say thank you.

For all of it.

For every joy,

every hardship,

every lesson,

every unknown.

Thank you, universe,

for letting me be here.

What a privilege it is to exist.

I did not choose to exist.

I did not ask to be here,

to wake up in this body,

in this time,

in this place.

But now that I am here,

I get to choose how I move,

how I breathe,

how I carve my path

through the shifting landscape of life.

I get to rebel against the darkness

with my joy,

with my laughter,

with the simple, defiant act

of being myself.

252

The world may try to press in,

to make itself heavier,

to crush me beneath its weight—

but I do not have to carry it.

I can let go.

I can breathe through it.

I can refuse to be buried.

Because I am not here

to be small,

to be silenced,

to be swallowed by the tide.

I am here to be free.

And so, I choose to exist

in a way that feels like me.

In a way that feels true,

that aligns with the rhythm of my soul.

I choose not to wait

for freedom to find me.

I will live it now.

I will breathe it into my body,

carry it in my movements,

let it guide my steps

toward a reality

where I am fully,

unapologetically,

free.

A brand new day begins to emerge.

Soft oranges spill first,
a warm, inviting glow,
stretching upward and outward,
reaching for the fire in my soul.

The light holds me,
its warmth seeping into my leaves,
its radiance woven into my veins.

Every hue greets the next,
as the day blooms from the night.

I marvel as the world awakens,
dew shimmering in the grass
like countless miniature suns,
scattering golden rays.

The air is heavy with moisture,

each droplet cradling light,

a liquid dance of brilliance

that nourishes all it touches.

When my body tells me it's time,

I release the tension at my flowers' base.

I bloom once again,

this time mirroring the moon.

As I unfurl my white crown,

I feel an intrinsic connection

to the world around me

My yellow petals are replaced

by white seedheads,

each one a tiny miracle.

Hundreds of stories waiting to begin.

I cradle them close,

feeling their downy softness

brush against each other

in the gentle morning breeze.

Each one precious,

each one carrying a spark

of my inner light,

of the universe's light.

I bask in the present moment,

embracing the gentle breeze

that carries whispers of distant adventures.

At night, when the moon rises,

full and luminous,

casting silver shadows across my crown,

I tuck in each seed

and tell them stories—

tales of shadows and light,

of underground journeys

and sky-bound flights.

I have waited for this moment.

It has taken everything to get here—
the slow stretching of my roots
into the unseen,
the gathering of sunlight in my leaves,
the resilience to stand tall
through trials that sought to break me.

I have known thirst and flood,
warmth and cold,
ease and pain.

I have bent but not broken.

I have reached for the sky
even when the weight of the earth
tried to pull me back down.

My roots anchor me firmly,

yet my essence stretches

far beyond my physical form.

My heartbeats align

with the rhythm of my roots,

my breath mingles

with the scent of rain and moss.

Things were never meant to be so complicated.

My only task is to soften my gaze,

to meet life as it is as I listen.

I stand here, still and unburdened,

letting the beauty of existence wash over me.

I release the need to strive,

the ceaseless quest to define and achieve.

Instead, I choose to inhabit this existence,
to breathe deeply, to simply be.

To roam the earth with my soul,
listening to the night's lullaby
sung by crickets and owls,
inhaling the scent of rain
mingled with pine and wildflowers,
feeling the breeze weave through my leaves,
embracing the warmth of the sun
as it pours over me like golden honey.

And perhaps that is everything.

To simply be—
an offering, a presence,
a soul at peace.

In this state of harmonious balance,

I sway effortlessly with life's rhythms.

I welcome each experience,

embracing all life has to offer,

sharing each moment with my seeds.

Contentment blooms within me.

Fully alive and attuned to my surroundings,

I greet each moment with an open heart

and a curious mind.

Challenges may rise,

but I face them with calm assurance,

knowing that answers will come,

or acceptance will follow.

True to myself,

I contribute to the ecosystem,

honoring the spark of creation

within all things.

My actions are gentle,

my growth steady,

a testament to the quiet power

of simply being.

With inner clarity,

I remain unshaken

by passing storms,

aware of life's transient nature.

I embrace change as my companion,

thriving in the eternal now,

where my essence blossoms

in unity with the universe.

As I stand adorned

with a crown of white seedheads,

I feel the gentle caress of the wind

coaxing me to let go.

Each breath of air invites my seeds

to embark on their own journeys.

Tiny vessels of possibility

tremble upon my stem,

eager to explore the world beyond.

My story is inscribed in each of them.

I once thought I was alone,

just a single stem in a field of gray,

fighting for space, for light, for life.

But now, I recognize

the soil cradling my roots

is the same earth

that nourishes all beings.

The wind that will carry my children away

is the same wind that once carried me here.

The sun that kissed me into bloom

has touched every leaf,

every petal,

every creature

that has ever lived on this surface.

Every element—

the storms,

the stillness,

the growth—

contributes to this narrative.

Each entity,

from towering trees

to fleeting insects,

from avian travelers

to fellow seeds,

composes its own chapter,

fulfilling its role

in the ever-evolving story of life.

We are all ink on the pages

of this infinite book,

a collection that spans beyond

what I can see,

beyond what I can understand.

And my contribution,

however small,

is meaningful.

I trust my seeds will find their way,

just as I have found mine.

I hold them up to the sun,

to the sky,

to the vastness beyond me.

They are my gift,

waiting to be carried into the unknown.

My seeds will not fall aimlessly.

They will land where they are meant to take root.

Some will soar across great distances,

carried by favorable winds,

while others may settle nearby,

finding fertile forests to grow in.

In both, there is purpose and promise.

And even those that do not bloom

will serve a purpose—

feeding the soil,

joining the endless cycle of life.

This is how it has always been.

For so long, I struggled,

taking every gust of wind as a threat,

every passing shadow as an omen.

I saw only the struggle,

the fight,

the need to survive.

But now, as I watch my seeds

dance with the breeze, I realize—

life is meant to be playful.

The unknown is not a void,

but a playground.

When I stop overthinking,

when I choose to see the world

with wonder instead of worry,

everything feels lighter.

The game is fun when I allow it to be.

I know every action has a reaction,

every seed carries a story,

and every story adds to the universe.

This story that we get to create

is an epic tale of countless adventures.

A new sound comes my way:

thump,

thump,

thump

thump.

The strong and steady,

rapidly approaching

footsteps of a creature.

A tall being bows to me,

blanketing me in shadows

as they pluck one of my seedheads

right off my stem.

The gentle tug

ripples through my body,

but I am not worried.

In letting go,

I find a new way to grow.

The creature summons a breath of wind

that catches my seeds,

lifting them high up above me.

They float upward,

scattering like white stars

against the soft blush

of the morning horizon,

each one carrying a fragment

of my love and light.

As they take flight,

their feathery pappi become parachutes

guiding them to new territories.

One by one, they drift away,

carried by the breeze.

I will miss them deeply

as they go on their journey.

Acknowledgements

To my wonderful spouse, thank you for helping me create a life where my inner light can truly shine. You've given me a home where I could find myself and grow into who I am meant to be. Your unwavering love and support have been a guiding force through this journey.

To the patient friends and family—both new and old—who have stood by me as I navigated my path, thank you. Your kindness and understanding have been a sanctuary, your belief in me a quiet strength that helped me keep going.

To the brilliant writers whose words have inspired me to build my own world—thank you for teaching me the magic of storytelling and the power of transformation. And to my time as a molecular biologist, which has deepened my connection to nature and influenced the way I see the world: I am grateful for the insight and perspective fellow scientists have provided.

A special thank you to my local Shut Up & Write group. Without your encouragement, accountability, and community, this book would never have been finished. You have been a gift in this process, and I am endlessly grateful.

Above all, thank you to the universe for allowing me to be here, to create, to grow, and to share my light with the world.

www.ingramcontent.com/pod-product-compliance
Lightning Source LLC
Chambersburg PA
CBHW072116270326
41931CB00010B/1576